Garrett '12 21.00

WHAT IS VALENTINE'S DAY?

Elaine Landau

Enslow Elementary
an imprint of
Enslow Publishers, Inc.
40 Industrial Road
Box 398
Berkeley Heights, NJ 07922
USA

http://www.enslow.com

CONTENTS

WORDS TO KNOW

cupid (KYOO pihd)—The Roman god of love. Cupid looks like a baby with wings. He is often seen with a bow and arrow.

lovebirds—Small birds that show caring for their mates.

symbol (SIHM buhl)— Something that stands for something else.

valentine—A card to show friendship or love.

3

WHAT A DAY!

What special day is this? There are flowers, greeting cards, and candy. Love and joy are in the air. It must be Valentine's Day!

5

A DAY FOR
CARING

It is a time for friends and
people we love. We think about
those who mean a lot to us.
We show them that we care.

WHO WAS ST. VALENTINE?

Some people say he was a priest who married young people. But the Roman ruler did not like this. He wanted young men to fight for him—not marry. On February 14, Valentine was put to death. We honor him on that day each year.

HEARTS, CUPIDS,
AND LOVEBIRDS

A symbol is something that stands for something else. Some Valentine's Day symbols are hearts, cupids, and lovebirds. They stand for love and happiness.

10

VALENTINE
CARDS

The cards we send
are called valentines.
You can make your
own cards or buy
them in stores.
Some cards are fancy.
Others are funny.

PARTIES
AND MORE

School classes may hang hearts and cupids in their rooms. They may have parties. Children give each other cards. Some schools have special plays that day.

FUN FOOD

Many people bake heart-shaped cakes. There are heart-shaped cookies and candies too. You can wash it all down with pink punch!

IT COMES EVERY YEAR

Valentine's Day has been around for hundreds of years. Many people enjoy this day each year. Is it one of your favorite times?

WHAT YOU CAN DO!

This Valentine's Day, show you really care. Send some special people a special valentine. Give them a "Caring Coupon."

You Will Need:
- ❖ paper
- ❖ crayons or pencils

What to Do:

- ❖ Decorate a sheet of paper with Valentine's Day symbols. On it, write something you will do for the person. A coupon for your mother might say:

This coupon is good for doing the dishes every Saturday for a month.

A coupon for your little brother might look like this:

This coupon is good for two hours of homework help.

A coupon for your grandmother might look like this:

This coupon is good for unlimited hugs and kisses.

Get the idea? Now make your own Caring Coupons for Valentine's Day.

Spread some love and joy!

LEARN MORE

BOOKS

Gibbons, Gail. *Valentine's Day Is . . . .* New York: Holiday House, 2006.

Haugen, Brenda. *Valentine's Day.* Mankato, Minn.: Picture Window Books, 2005.

Boonyadhistarn, Thiranut. *Valentines: Cards and Crafts from the Heart.* Mankato, Minn.: Capstone Press, 2006.

Trueit, Trudi Strain. *Valentine's Day.* New York: Children's Press, 2007.

WEB SITES

Sponge Heart Valentines Card

<http://www.enchantedlearning.com/crafts/valentine/spongeheartcard/>

Valentine's Day Activities for Kids

<http://www.dltk-holidays.com/valentines/index.htm>

INDEX

Enslow Elementary, an imprint of Enslow Publishers, Inc.

Enslow Elementary® is a registered trademark of Enslow Publishers, Inc.

Copyright © 2012 by Elaine Landau

Library of Congress Cataloging-in-Publication Data

Landau, Elaine.
   What is Valentine's Day? / by Elaine Landau.
     p. cm. — (I like holidays!)
   Includes bibliographical references and index.
   Summary: "Provides information about how Valentine's Day is
celebrated, popular symbols of the holiday, and a brief history.
A Valentine's Day activity is included"—Provided by publisher.
   ISBN 978-0-7660-3699-4
   1. Valentine's Day—Juvenile literature. I. Title.
   GT4925.L37 2012
   394.2618—dc22   2010006293

Paperback ISBN 978-1-59845-296-9

Printed in China
052011 Leo Paper Group, Heshan City, Guangdong, China
10 9 8 7 6 5 4 3 2 1

Photo Credits: iStockphoto.com: © Amanda Dumouchelle, p.18, © Ana
Abejon, p. 3 (middle), © daniel rodriguez, p. 7, © Judy Barranco, p. 11,
© Mike Sonnenberg, p. 2; © Mary Kate Denny /PhotoEdit, p. 12; © North
Wind Picture Archives /Alamy, p. 8; © Photos.com, p. 4; Shutterstock.com,
pp. 1, 3 (top and bottom), 10 (both), 13, 15, 16, 17, 19, 21, 22, 23, 24.

Cover Photo: Shutterstock.com

Series Consultant:
Duncan R. Jamieson, PhD
Professor of History
Ashland University
Ashland, OH

Series Literacy Consultant:
Allan A. De Fina, PhD
Dean, College of Education/Professor of
    Literacy Education
New Jersey City University
Past President of the New Jersey Reading Association